ADVENTURE TIME™

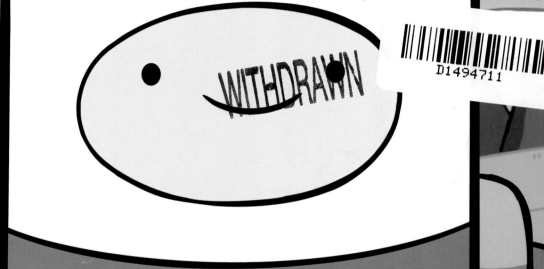

FINN'S HEROIC QUEST

SEARCH-AND-FIND

WITHDRAWN

PUFFIN BOOKS

UK | USA | Canada | Ireland | Australia
India | New Zealand | South Africa

Puffin Books is part of the Penguin Random House group of
companies whose addresses can be found at
global.penguinrandomhouse.com.

puffinbooks.com

Penguin
Random House
UK

First published 2015
001

Made and printed in China

ISBN: 978–0–141–35873–4

Contents

Dude, you gotta help me out!

My best bro, Jake, is missing somewhere in the Land of Ooo. We were doing some regular adventuring, just like always, when suddenly **BAM!** Jake had disappeared!

I'm a pretty mathematical adventurer and I could totally find him by myself. But Jake might be in trouble so I've gotta work super quick – and that's why I need your help! If we search together, I know we'll find him WAY FASTER.

In each kingdom of Ooo, see if you can spot Jake amongst all the citizens and other banaynays stuff. And remember – he's so stretchy he could be any shape and size!

Thanks for the help, fellow adventurer. You're the raddest.

Finn

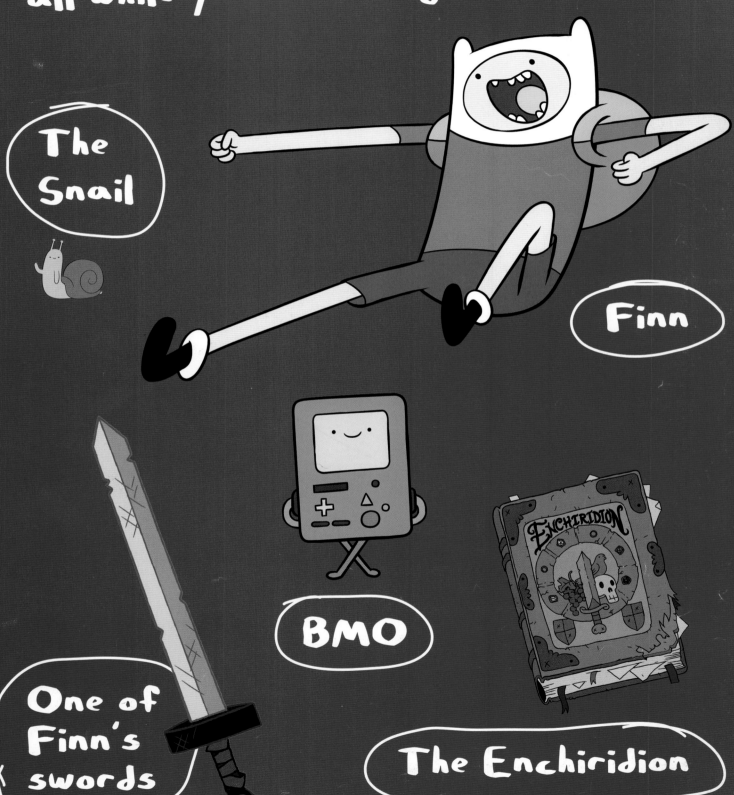

CANDY KINGDOM

Ruled by Princess Bubblegum, the Candy Kingdom is a really sweet place to go adventuring. In fact, Finn and Jake were hanging out right next to the Candy Castle when Jake went missing! Can you spot him amongst the sugary citizens?

COTTON CANDY MAZE

Jake's paw prints look like they're heading into the Cotton Candy Forest! Can you draw a line through the maze to help Finn navigate amongst the trees?

START

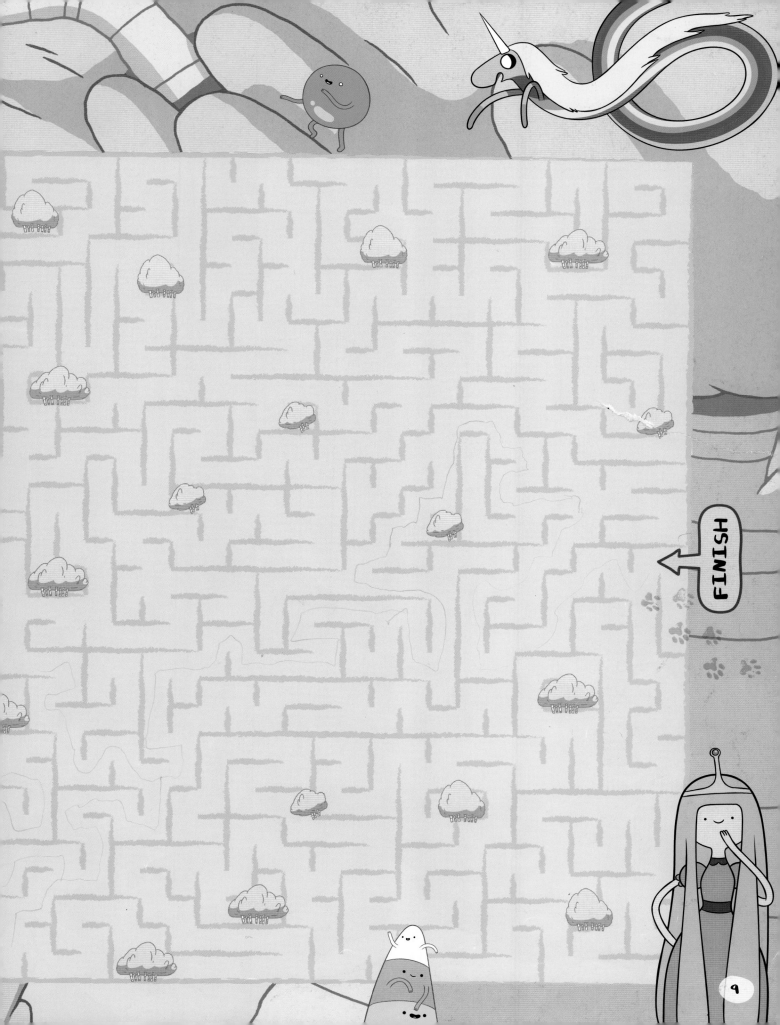

FINISH

9

LUMPY SPACE

While walking through the Cotton Candy Forest, Finn took a detour via frog guts into Lumpy Space! Lumpy Space Princess and all the other lumpers are heading over to Promcoming right now – but is Jake going with them? See if you can spot him in the crowd.

LUMPY SEQUENCES

How good are you at spotting stuff? Test your skills by looking at these sequences of lumpers on their way to Promcoming. Which lumper should come next in each row? Draw each one in the circle when you work it out!

SPACE WORD SEARCH

There are twelve things from Lumpy Space hidden in the grid below. Can you use your spotting skills to find them all? Then see if you can find each thing in the Lumpy Space scene on pages ten and eleven as well!

CROWN
PRINCESS
TIN OF BEANS
CLOUDS
STAR
BRAD

CAR
MELISSA
LUMPY SPACE QUEEN
JAKE
FINN
ANTIDOTE

T E H U C W Y S P H I O O O N
M G I T I N O F B E A N S R N
Q O F X T I D Q G R J V S R A S
U Y J I H T W C A U A O R T P Y
S W A X N X I P R I N C E S Y S
X V K Z G N W X S L P J S M R S
N E E U Q E C A P S Y P M U T L
D S V C R O W N D A N L C Z A E
A L P Q U M Z K E N V A M T D Q
E Z R E L U B Q P T N C M Z E D
L T X V X N R J T I Z P Y M Q G
M W D Z T S A G A D N I N X A J
F S J P Y P D C L O U D S L R J
T M E L I S S A Y T Q F F R C P
Y B O Z T L F N M E F B A E P

MARCELINE'S HOUSE

Maybe the baddest Vampire Queen in Ooo knows where Jake is . . . Finn has travelled to Marceline's cave to find out. BIG MISTAKE. Marceline has raised an army of the dead and the cave is overrun with skeletons! Can you see Jake anywhere amongst these bony folk?

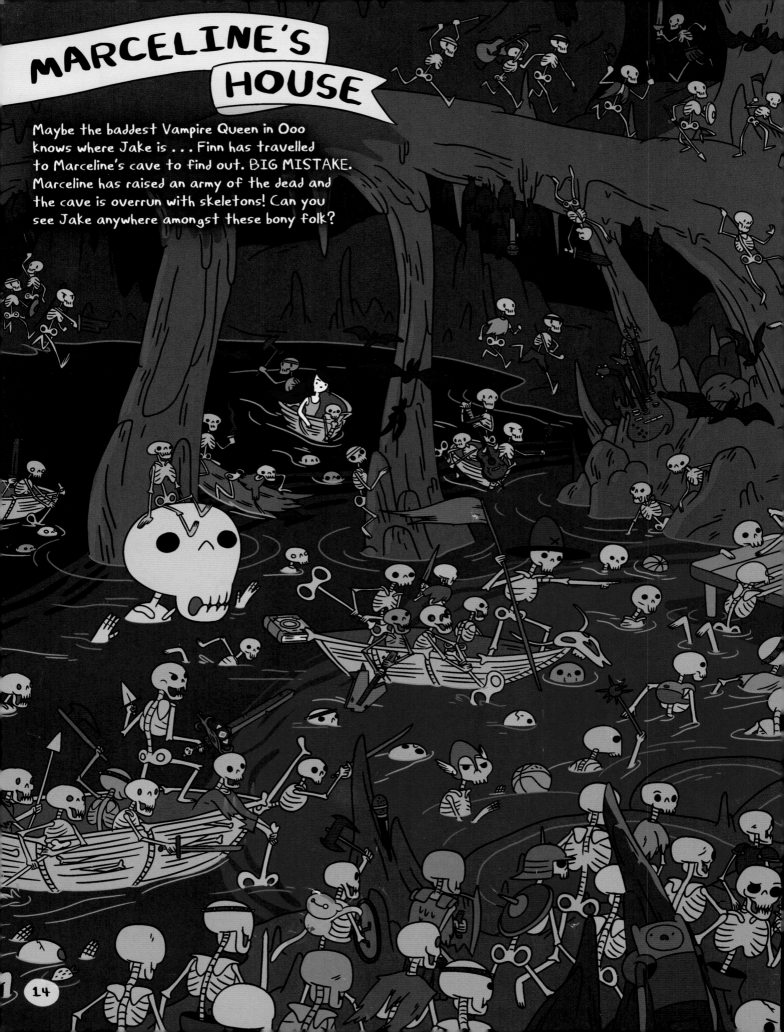

SCARY SPOT THE DIFFERENCE

Marceline is a radical dame, but she sure can be scary. Can you spot fifteen differences between these two pictures of Marcy and her undead pals?

CLOUD KINGDOM

If there's one thing Jake loves to do, it's party. There's an awesome party going on in the Cloud Kingdom right now and it looks like everyone in Ooo has been invited! Can you spot Jake anywhere in this crazy-sweet scene?

CLOUD CHECKLIST

Think you got a good look at the Cloud Kingdom just now? Look at the checklist below, then find one of each item in the scene on pages eighteen and nineteen.

Books

Yellow T-shirt

Blue radio

Barrel

Can of soda

Pink vase

Bongo drums

Baseball bat

Green sunglasses

Red flag

Purple vase

American football

CLOUD CODE

To help Finn on his quest, the Party God has given him a coded message. Can you help him decipher the note, using the key below?

The deciphered message reads:

JAKE WENT TO THE FIRE KINGDOM. THAT GUY CAN REALLY PARTY!

FIRE KINGDOM

Finn's search for his pal Jake is heating up. He's travelled to the Fire Kingdom – a toasty place ruled by his hot-headed friend, Flame Princess. She's got all sorts of Flame People hanging around her fiery palace, but is Jake anywhere in the crowd?

23

LAVA MAZE

Looks like Jake has already escaped the Fire Kingdom – so it's time for Finn to make a speedy exit, too! Can you draw a line to guide Finn along the paths to the finish? Watch out for the boiling lava!

START

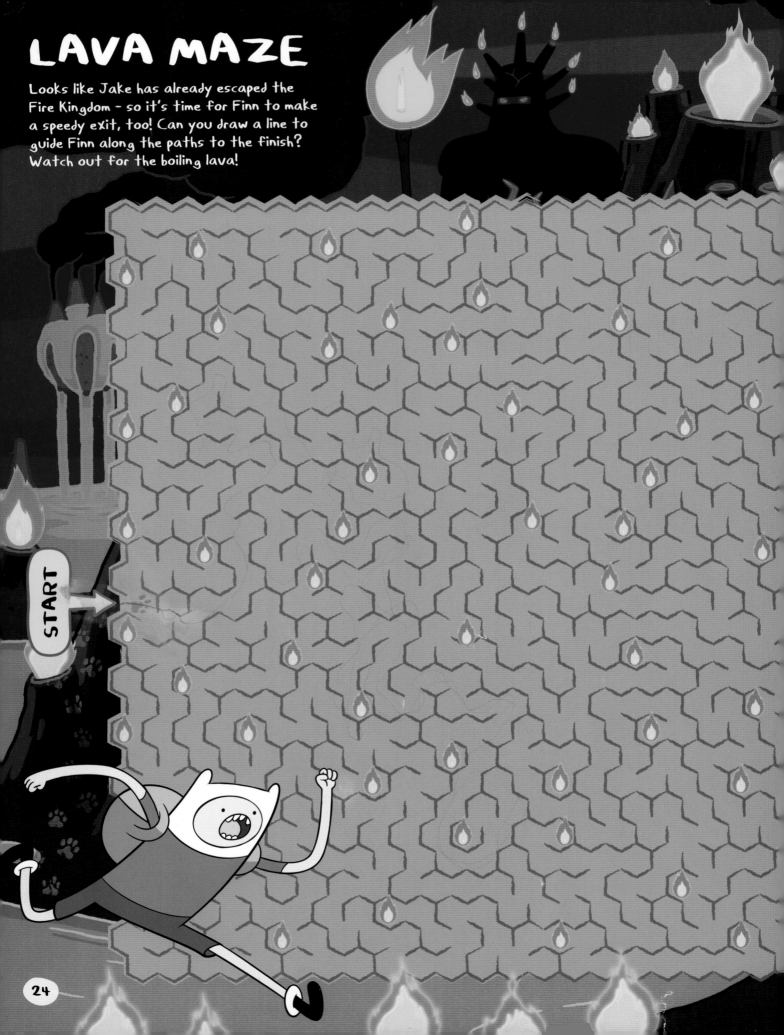

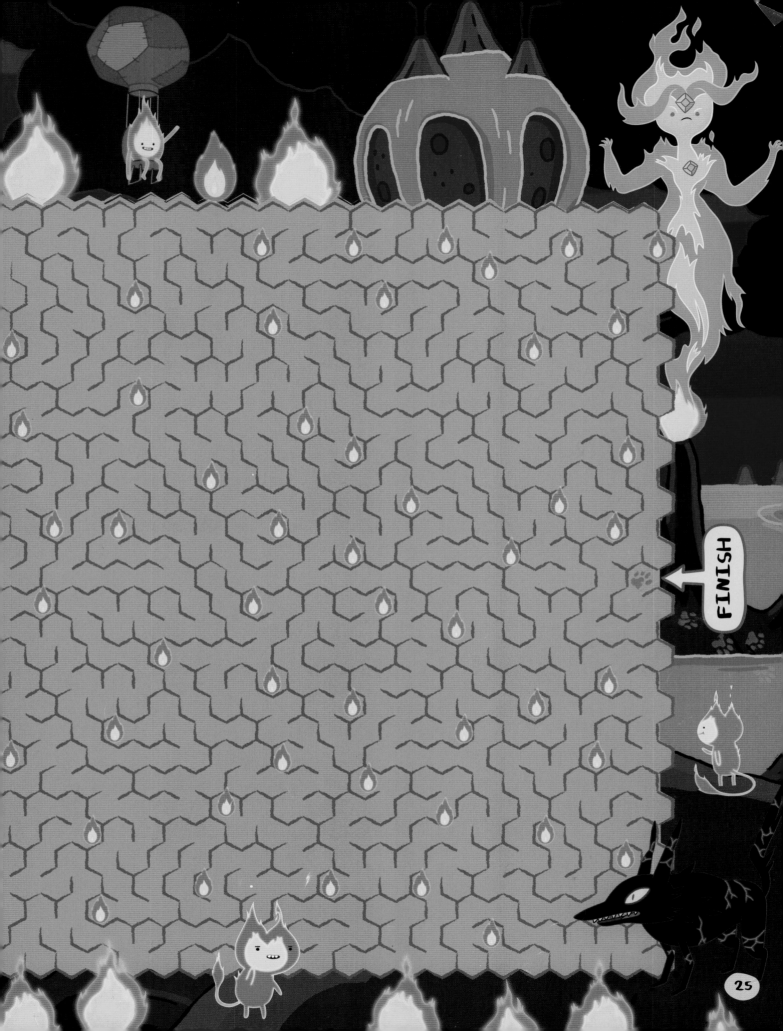

FINISH

25

EVIL FOREST

Uh-oh. Finn's quest to find Jake has taken him to one of the scariest places in Ooo: THE EVIL FOREST! Mean-looking trees, zombies that look like signposts, butterflies with creepy skull-heads . . . Is Jake anywhere to be seen in this terrifying place?

EVIL WORD SEARCH

Spotting skills at the ready, adventurer! There are twelve things from the Evil Forest hidden in the grid below. Can you find them all? See if you can spot them in the Evil Forest scene on pages twenty-six and twenty-seven, too!

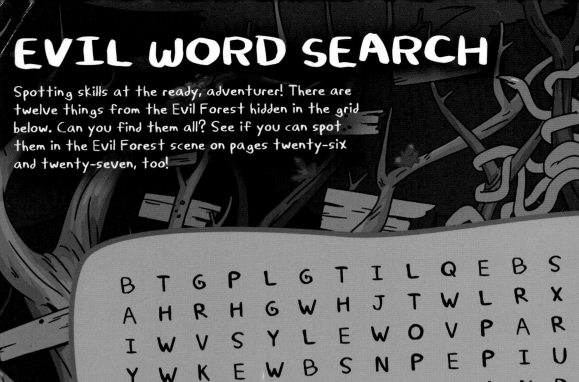

```
B T G P L G T I L Q E B S Q V
A H R H G W H J T W L R X H S
I W V S Y L E W O V P A R M O
Y W K E W B S N P E P I U N I
L K O L P I N L A K A N D Q I
F N B F A K A R E A M B A T Y
R P U F N M I O T J E E S R T
E Z G O Y U L S H D G A B E E
T E U L X K L L Z J L S E E K
K G L H E Z B Z S A T Z T S A
U A W A S R E K C I T S R R A
B J V W A Y N W N V S T J U B
T O A D S T O O L Z Y B N N V
I S V A G V N T Z U R O U K D
T E K N A L B U U E C N X S L
```

TREE TRUNKS
BRAIN BEAST
CRYSTAL GEM APPLE
THE SNAIL
WALL OF FLESH
TOADSTOOL

BUTTERFLY
STICKERS
TEAPOT
BASKET
BLANKET
JAKE

EVIL CLOSE-UPS

Here's another test to see how beady-eyed you are, bro. The twelve images below are close-ups from the Evil Forest on pages twenty-six and twenty-seven. Can you spot each one in the bigger scene? Tick the boxes as you find them!

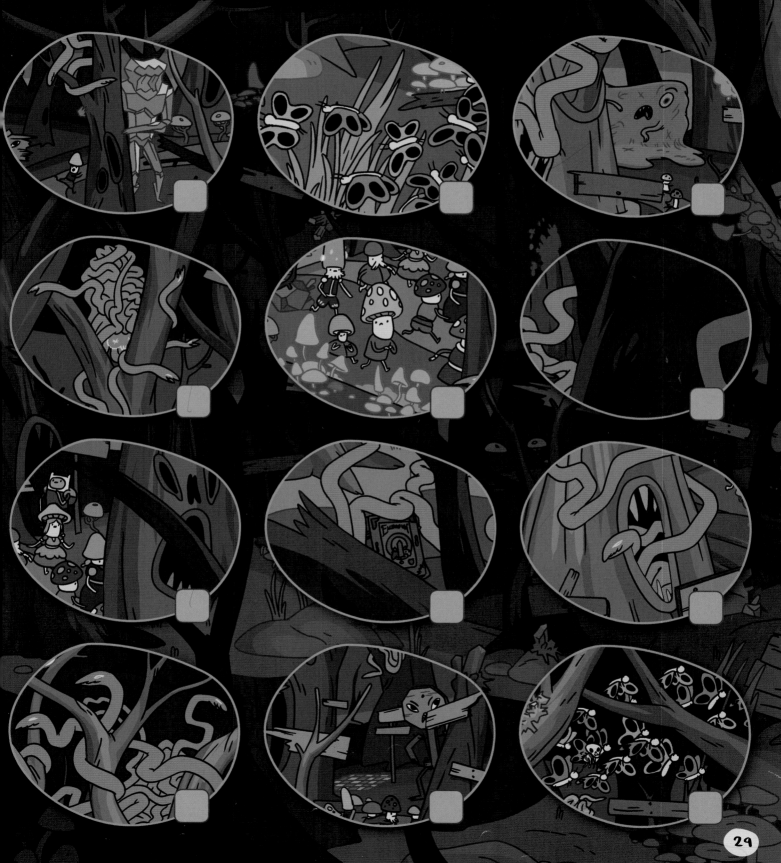

ICE KINGDOM RESCUE

There's one c-c-c-cold place that Finn hasn't been to yet on his quest . . . and that's the Ice Kingdom. That sneaky dude the Ice King is always up to something suspicious. Sure enough, Jake is here, as well as hundreds of Gunters! Can you see where Jake is hiding?

SPOT THE DIFFERENCE, DUDE

Good work finding Jake, adventurer! Now look at these two pictures of the Ice Kingdom and see if you can spot fifteen differences between them.

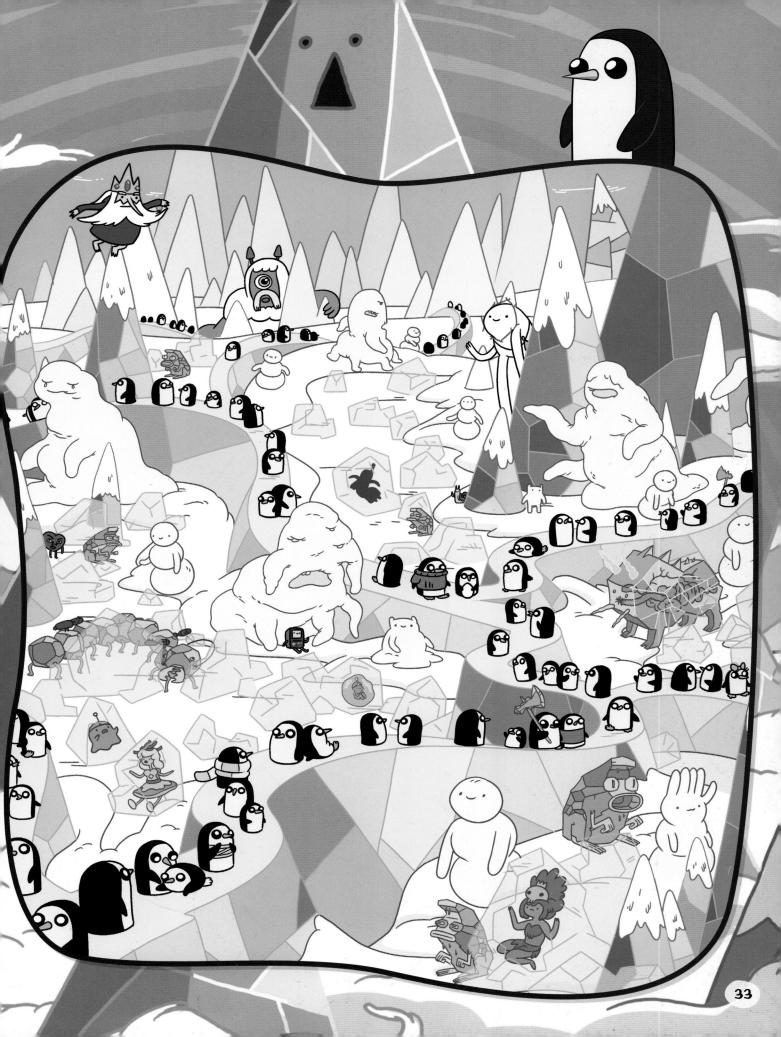

TREE FORT PARTY!

Turns out the Ice King didn't capture Jake after all! Jake smelled bacon cooking in the Ice King's kitchen, then followed his super-strength nose all the way to the Ice Kingdom to get it! Now that the best bros have been reunited, it's time to celebrate. See if you can spot Finn and Jake having a rad time in this rhombus party scene!

MORE TO FIND . . .

CANDY KINGDOM

- Princess Bubblegum
- Peppermint Butler
- Science the rat
- PB's laboratory flask
- Dr Ice Cream
- Four marshmallow kids
- Two Candy Guards
- Two Gumdrop Lasses

LUMPY SPACE

- Lumpy Space Princess
- LSP's house
- Lumpy Space King
- Glasses
- Monty
- Lenny
- LSP's purse
- Five tins of beans
- Four bright green lumpers

MARCELINE'S HOUSE

- Marceline
- Hambo
- Two-toned shield
- Axe bass
- Fender bass
- Butterfly bass

- ☐ Devil Monster bass
- ☐ Lunatic bass
- ☐ Acoustic guitar
- ☐ Banjolele
- ☐ Four microphones
- ☐ Two amplifiers
- ☐ Five basketballs
- ☐ Four white strawberries

CLOUD KINGDOM

- ☐ Party God
- ☐ Cloud house
- ☐ Cinnamon Bun
- ☐ Starchy
- ☐ Peppermint Butler
- ☐ Pineapple Guy

- ☐ Five barrels
- ☐ Four ladybirds
- ☐ Four red flags
- ☐ Six water nymphs
- ☐ CMO

FIRE KINGDOM

- ☐ Flame Princess
- ☐ Cinnamon Bun
- ☐ Flame King
- ☐ Flambo
- ☐ Jalapĕno Pepper

- ☐ Furnius
- ☐ Torcho
- ☐ Mr Pig
- ☐ Four flame drawings
- ☐ Three skulls

EVIL FOREST

- [ ] Crystal Guardian
- [ ] Five Sign Zombies
- [ ] Four teacups
- [ ] Three scary-looking rocks
- [ ] Ten green toadstools
- [ ] Ten red toadstools

ICE KINGDOM RESCUE

- [ ] Ice King
- [ ] Ice King's castle
- [ ] Gunthelina
- [ ] Snow Golem
- [ ] Princess Bubblegum
- [ ] Wildberry Princess
- [ ] Space Angel Princess
- [ ] Gridface Princess
- [ ] Slime Princess
- [ ] Jungle Princess

- [ ] Ice-o-pede
- [ ] Ice Bull
- [ ] Iceclops
- [ ] Ricardio
- [ ] Kitten
- [ ] Kitten's egg
- [ ] Breakfast Princess
- [ ] Embryo Princess
- [ ] Eight Ice Toads

TREE FORT PARTY!

- [ ] Finn and Jake dancing together
- [ ] Lady Rainicorn
- [ ] Shelby
- [ ] Cinnamon Bun
- [ ] Starchy
- [ ] Banana Man
- [ ] Neptr
- [ ] Tree Trunks

- [ ] Choose Goose
- [ ] Princess Bubblegum
- [ ] Marceline
- [ ] Ice King
- [ ] Lumpy Space Princess
- [ ] Pink crystal
- [ ] Five rainbows

Thanks for helping me find Jake, man! You're the most **algebraic** finder of stuff I ever met.

Totally agreed, bro. TRUST POUND!

ANSWERS

Pages 8-9: Cotton Candy Maze

Page 12: Lumpy Sequences

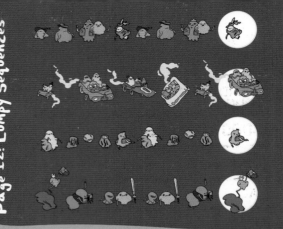

Pages 16-17: Scary Spot the Difference

Page 13: Space Word Search

```
T E H U C W Y S P H I O O O N
M G I T I N O F B E A N S R A
Q O F X T I D Q g R J V S P S
U Y J I H T W C A U A O R T Y
S W A X N X I P R I N C E S S
X V K Z G N W X S L P J S M R
N E E U Q E C A P S Y P M U L
D S V C R O W N A N L C T A E
A L P Q U M Z K E N V A M Z D
E Z R E L U B Q P T N C S Z D
L T V X N R A J T I Z P Y M Q
M W D Z J T S A G D N I N X A
F T S J F P S Z I C L A L G J
T Y M E L I S S A Y T Q F M C
Y B O Z T L F N M E V E B A E P
```

Page 28: Evil Word Search

```
B T G P L G T I L Q E B S Q V
A H R H G W H J T W L P A X H
I W V S Y L E W O V E P R M O
L W K E W B S N P E P A U N Q
N K O L P I N L A K A M B E A
F R E P U F N M I O T J A M B
E T Z G O Y U L S H D G E A S
E L L X K L L Z J L S B E B E
T K G L H E Z B Z S A T R E T
U B A W A S R E K C I T S A B
O V W A Y N W N V S T J U N K
T O A D S T O O L Z Y B N B V
I S V A G V N T Z U R O U X D
T E K N A L B U U E C N X S L
```

Page 21: Cloud Code
Jake went to the Fire Kingdom.
That guy can really party!

Pages 24-25: Lava Maze

Pages 32-33: Spot the Difference, Dude